TOWARDS A GENERAL THEORY OF LOVE

Clare Shaw was born in Burnley in 1972. Her first two collections with Bloodaxe were *Straight Ahead* (2006), which was shortlisted for the Glen Dimplex New Writers' Award for Poetry and attracted a Forward Prize Highly Commended for Best Single Poem, and *Head On* (2012), which according to the *Times Literary Supplement* is 'fierce, memorable and visceral'. Her later collections are *Flood* (2018), a New Writing North Read Regional title in 2019, and *Towards a General Theory of Love* (2022), written after winning a Northern Writers' Award.

She is co-director of Kendal Poetry Festival, a Royal Literary Fund Project Fellow, and a regular tutor for Wordsworth Grasmere and Arvon. She also works as a mental health trainer and has taught and published widely in the field, including *Our Encounters with Self-Injury* (eds. Baker, Biley and Shaw, PCCS, 2013) and *Otis Doesn't Scratch* (PCCS, 2015), a unique storybook resource for children who live with self-injury. Along with the novelist Winnie M Li, Clare was the recipient of a Royal Society of Literature Literature Matters award in 2019, creating workshops and an online resource for survivors of trauma. In 2021, she co-wrote and presented *Four Ways to Weather the Storm* for BBC Radio Four, examining the relationship between creativity, landscape and resilience. Clare lives above Hebden Bridge with her daughter and their pet rat.

CLARE SHAW

Towards a General
Theory of Love

BLOODAXE BOOKS

ISBN: 978 1 78037 604 2

First published 2022 by
Bloodaxe Books Ltd,
Eastburn,
South Park,
Hexham,
Northumberland NE46 1BS.

www.bloodaxebooks.com
For further information about Bloodaxe titles
please visit our website and join our mailing list
or write to the above address for a catalogue

Supported using public funding by
**ARTS COUNCIL
ENGLAND**

Cover design: Neil Astley & Pamela Robertson-Pearce.

Printed in Great Britain by Bell & Bain Limited, Glasgow, Scotland, on
acid-free paper sourced from mills with FSC chain of custody certification.

Love, and the lack of it, changes the young brain forever.

LEWIS, AMINI AND LANNON, *A General Theory of Love*

The effects of 6 months of total social isolation were so devastating and debilitating that we had assumed initially that 12 months of isolation would not produce any additional decrement. This assumption proved to be false.

HARLOW, *Total social isolation in monkeys*

CONTENTS

What the Frog Taught Me About Love

Owl says look very hard for it.
Turkey says dance very well for it.

Goose says just be born to it.
Dog says roll yourself in it,

be governed by fear of loss of it.
Cat says you can always leave.

Chimp says you have to fight for it.
Lamb says leap for the joy of it.

Wolf says howl for it. Die for it.
Monkey goes mad for the lack of it.

Bowerbird says go to great lengths for it.
Penguin walks hundreds of miles for it.

Firefly burns very bright for it.
Frog just holds on. Tight.

Letter to My Mother

I have a daughter, you'd like my partner. I'm doing well in the ways that count. As for the news – it's late and the light's too faint for writing. Just tell me about yourself, the things that matter: how many skips of a stone you could make on the water; the roses; the nameless trees. Let's leave all the bad stuff to one side. Talk about Mass, the tide of the voices. How words were a river – tell me what it was like to be seized by a river. Tell me about your God. Tell me when you were most yourself.

Tell me about your garden – how did it feel when the stones fell out from your walls, when the path faded, when your world softened and lost its edges? When you were broken and couldn't be mended, when the words got stuck in your throat – how did it feel when people were ghosts and you wouldn't wear glasses, when you got lost, when world was all losses?

Now tell me birdsong and flowers. Tell me the importance of very good manners. Do you remember the Lakes? Do you visit? Do you recall how high the grass grew, how it was sweet at the roots? Can you taste it?

It's late. Can you open your eyes? Can you speak? Can you tell me before the light goes out completely?

Elegy for My Grandma

I want to write about birds in her garden,
pear trees, high hedges. How soft her cheek was,
how her hair was still black in her eighties,
how thick hair runs in our genes

and the picture of Croagh Patrick on her wall
and her in the photo
back for the summer and harvest in Mayo,
her deep smile, her eyes all lazy –

the millionaire's proposal she turned down
and what made her laugh though I can't remember
and how when she sang
she was high and quavery

and the taste of hot milk before bed, two biscuits –
how I woke up to song from the garden
and her out on the lawn in the early morning,
dark hair, dark eyes, black as a raven

and all the sin in her smile
and the kettles she filled to break ice in the winter,
and the teas that she served to the men in the prison
and the sun through the open door.

Not the lost purse ripped sheet wet skirt
smashed plate the windows broken
how she was a joke and not one person was laughing
she ruined the greenhouse

she locked all the doors
she was an argument not worth having
she was a thief she was nothing but hungry
she was a girl all at sea.

She was a sick bird and no one could help her
then she was a blizzard and no one could find her
then she was a climber
and no one could hold her

and we watched her falling for years.
Then she was a field
with no footprints in it.
The silence of snow. No one there.

abcedarian

aphasia is an inability to formulate l anguage due to
braindama ge caused by a
complex   intera ction   of cerebrovascular
  disease and risk factors   you can' t
even name   your losses   sometimes they feel like
 fire   does it hurt there were
  girls on my wa llpaper holding
hands   but i don' t have a dictionary
   i don't have a   map and   when you can't
join th e dots   there is no cure
kiddo   all you have
 left is dots   she was my
   mother no story can hold this   the decli
ne happened stepby step and
           ogoditwasterrible
  progressive   is not the right word   but
quite what it is   is beyond me   did it hu
 rt when she didn t remember you   or the
standardised or der ing ofle tt ers   sh e was my m o
        th er shesounded like in a dre am or
und er w ate r she was l os t shewas
      very tired   idontremember her last
 words   shewas sleeping in the ne
 xt room   on a scale of 1-10   didit hurt
yes ten
zillion

The Night Your Mother Died

If you couldn't say how afraid you were
you'd make a storm.

Warnings would be issued on the coast:
a risk of flooding.

It would be dark, of course,
and you'd call it Erik.

If you had no words for it,
the wind would howl

and the windmills would be frantic
by the road.

There would be no owl,
no ground to stand on.

The wind would be black wings beating,
they'd knock you breathless.

Because you couldn't tell anyone
there'd be no moon.

Fences would be broken,
trees would fall.

There'd be no other cars on the road
and the moor would be empty.

If you couldn't say how alone you were
there'd be the moor.

This is a very small poem

it starts with a single image

the room where she laid for years
there are photos of me on the wall   a knitted shawl

it doesn't squander a word
it was cold and the wind was howling   I was shaking
I did not turn away

there is nothing of excess here   no drama
there was blood on her cheeks   I could not help her
no adverbs   I thanked her
she could not close her eyes

I am keeping this short   I had my coat on
I was leaving   I kissed her
I could not hear the storm

                I wished her freedom
her shoulders were heaving   she was breathing
very loudly

        then she wasn't

I didn't know what to do

I am saying it quickly
it was remarkable it was terrible
I had my head   on the bed   I was panting   they left me
        alone   she was gone

I have counted every syllable of this
I was calling her name

oh mum I feel nothing

her hands were so soft

I can still hear the screaming
it is elegant in its restraint

An Empirical Examination of the Stage Theory of Grief

The silence of lakes. Rain in the evening.
The music has stopped and the people are leaving.
Her face was a shadow. The sound of her breathing.

Blood on her cheeks. The house we once lived in.
The scars I'd forgotten. The junk in the garden.
Empty cafés. Her eyes were wide open.

Ash on the table. The glasses are empty.
The fire has gone out and the carpet is dirty.
A girl all alone and her friends at the party.

Three in the morning. An old woman singing.
The wind on the moor. The smell of stale urine.
Motorway driving. The heavy rain falling.

The stars are all out and there's light on the water.
A small patch of dirt in the shape of my mother.
The flowers are dead and the summer is over.

Morecambe Bay as Grief

Grief is the negative image of love, and if there can be an
accumulation of love over the years, then why not of grief?

JULIAN BARNES

If you leave a bath tap running
for twenty million years, it will drain the bay.
The otters have never left and there are seals,

an abundance of special birds.
You can visit, but you must love mud.
And nostalgia. Keep an eye on the time.

People work the sands at night
for little pay.
The geese will fly overhead

and there are sunsets.
I don't know how many gallons
it holds, but the skies are endless.

You will be in company, though it is desolate.
The sand may be warm.
It is entirely unpredictable

it is treacherous, people have died here.
Except you might take off your shoes,
you might have chips.

There is quicksand, everyone knows this. But not
everyone. Your daughter could stand by its side.
You could teach her

how to skim stones. It is a serious undertaking.
There is kindness here, and many hotels.
You will need a guide.

The signs warn of fast-rising tides.
The arcades may be open. The sands are shifting.
It is prettier than you expect.

The sandbanks may shine in the sun, there are curlews.
If you leave two bath taps running,
it will only take ten million years.

Monkey Writes a Poem About His Mother

(after Billy Collins)

> The children who really suffered, the little monkeys
> who wholly grieved, were the ones who felt they
> had lost something.
>
> DEBORAH BLUM

You were the seed and the leaf and the fruit.
You were the earth and you were the root.

You were the song in the echoing dark.
You were not snake. You were never the rock.

You were needle and bark, and you were the river.
You were not winter. You were fresh water.

You were not locked door or slammed door or rattle.
You were not metal. You were not empty bottle.

You were treetop and grassland and night sky and star.
Oh you were warm, you were rain, you were air.

You were the oak leaf and honey and clover
and you were the forest and you were my mother.

You were the shore where no crocodiles are.
You were not wire. You were not wire.

Rhosymedre: Prelude on a Welsh Hymn

It's all in there: how soft her feet were
after years of not walking, how her breath was so loud
it was like she was speaking.
How the cello can hold it, how I couldn't believe it,
it was more than a person could bear –

how we woke to the sound of the stream
in the garden, how weeping endures
and joy comes in the morning,
how loss is a church and the heart is an organ.
How pain can be sunlight; how grief is white blossom.

How we were star, oh the sobbing viola,
the wonder of it and the bluebells and horror,
how grief is a lake I will walk by forever –
oh the love that was summer,
my mother, my mother.

The Day Thou Gavest

In her final minutes,
there was horror.
The world shrank to the size of her room

and her bed was an altar.
It's not that she finally returned
but she was my mother

like I'd not understood
before. She was absolute wonder,
she was magic and power:

the blast in the dark,
the black ocean
where all life began.

I wasn't afraid to look
though her eyes were bloody
and her feet were horribly cold.

It's been a year since she died
and she hasn't visited.
She has never appeared in my dreams.

What did I imagine –
that she'd come back
to a quiet stream in the sun

and she'd be whole?
Death was her final act
and I accept it

though the voice of prayer
is never silent,
nor dies the strain of praise away.

Lesbian Conception in the Euston Hilton

There was no god
only a barman who served me juice
and football on the screen in the corner.

When the moon rose over the city
I slept alone.
No sea without shore

and no waves breathing.
In the morning
nobody sang.

There was no Big Bang.
The telly was on next door
and the birds were awake.

I watched squirrels in a park
and drank coffee
and nothing at all

felt the same. It was there.
It was one cell dividing.
A light rain was falling

and the trees were already green.

Midwife, Calderdale General Hospital

In the beginning,
I was carbon
pressed by forces

I could not imagine
and nothing I could do
would change it

and then I was on the floor;
there was something not right
in the water –

the rush and the torment of car
and the hours without respite
or reason.

The winter moon rose at three.
You, midnight sentry
keeping watch over acres of pain –

I cannot remember your name
though whatever tide took me,
you were there.

You made me a lake to drift in
and all was well. Water held me.
There were trees,

lights hung in them
and the ceiling was skies
and my music was playing

and someone was kissing my head.
I was holy
and going to make it,

in the beautiful pool,
in the pull;
me

suffering in the old life
without my baby;
in the same dark world

where all natural light had died
save the stars in the icy skies.
There were streetlights on empty roads

and a low glow hung over the town –
the day not yet broken
and her not yet born

and the end still before us and all the beginnings
and there on that ward,
the lights were all blazing.

Nocturne for My Daughter

The night is a sea
and you are a furious storm.
I can do nothing to calm you.

Fox shrieks,
owl is sleepless.
Forest breathes in the darkness.

Rage makes you strong.
The breast is a moon
and it scares you.

You did not ask to be born.
Sleep
runs through me like stone,

I can hardly move.
We watch films
we will never remember

and you are warm,
your shoulder tucked under
my chin.

Stars fade.
The room comes into focus.
My feet make no sound

on the carpet.
I hold you like fruit
in my palm.

The day is upon us –
its early grey light
and its music:

the first birds singing.
Two or three cars on the road.

This Is About My Mother

And the fox will find his feet,
rabbits will startle. The hare
will gather his legs beneath him.

There will be no blood.
Hedgehogs will hurry in hundreds
to the verge

where the badger will bare
her teeth. The cat will blink
dust from her eyes

and an old dog grow warm
in the sun, push his nose again
into your palm.

He'll race like a flame for the field
where the grouse will call
her own name. Come back.

The owl will peel his feathers
from the tar
and his wings will be wind,

whilst a squirrel runs for the trees
light as smoke.
The roe deer will rise

with the sun, unbroken –
that quick flash of light
in the ferns.

You won't see her.
But when the fawn cries for her mother
she will come.

Child Protection Policy

Once, everything felt like threat.
Only my body could keep yours
alive.

I'd get up to check your breathing:
it was shallow and warm on my cheek
and the whole world swam in its tide.

I stared into the dark
where no monsters were,
built fences to keep you safe,

put the matches on the highest shelf.
I took on the wolf
with my own weak teeth.

Never will you not be my child,
would I not hold you,
wrap you in blankets of stars,

sweep stones from your path
so you won't fall.
I will hold your hand by habit on the road.

And you ask, would I die for you?
A thousand times over.
But the fences are growing smaller

and you should climb them.
I am giving you the matches.
Now make fire.

A Psychological Study of The Strange Situation

Tonight, I want to talk about attachment
but Monkey is quiet
so we park near the woods in the dark.

This snow has been falling for days
and the track is white.
The trees are tall and black

against the sky.
I'm afraid of the ice, but Monkey
scampers ahead on all fours.

He looks back.
Monkey, I say, you seem happy.
He grunts very quietly.

I'm aware he is partly wild.
There only sound here is the river.
Nobody knows where we are.

There's no moon
but the path is bright.
We carry on walking, snow falling.

He places his paw in mine.

Monkey and I Discuss the Difficulty of Working Therapeutically with Non-verbal Traumatic Memories

When the monkeys were moved, they were so 'enormously disturbed' that two of them refused to eat and starved themselves to death.

DEBORAH BLUM

If I could put words to it, says Monkey,
that would be half the problem solved.

Poor Monkey. All he can do is scream
and that is unsatisfying.

He is not convinced by bodywork
and he doesn't like dancing.

Perhaps you could draw me your story, I suggest,
but he eats the pen.

Why are you frowning? asks Monkey.
He seems concerned.

Perhaps he could mime me the little cage
where he was kept

or express his alonenesss with sand.
It ends badly.

We are trying so hard to reach each other
but his body spells fear.

Language is over-rated, I tell Monkey
but he won't believe me.

If I can't tell you my story, he says,
I'll live there alone.

Give me your hand, little Monkey.
Come look at the moon

But his eyes are an empty sky right now
and his face is an empty room.

My Bedroom

I am walking through the rooms
in my old house.
There are many of them.

There are creatures who never see light;
they depend on great pressure.
I am telling you this for no reason.

If you leave a baby long enough,
it learns not to cry.
I am standing at the threshold

to my room.
The carpet is green.
Shall we go back downstairs?

We can get warm
in front of the fire,
we can scorch our shins.

Not everything is in shadow –
I could read in the faintest of lights
and there were trees.

Most creatures will learn to adapt,
most can swim.
A chest of drawers. Are we done?

You'd be surprised
what a human can bear
or maybe you wouldn't.

My dolls were silent,
they had marks on their faces

An account of my reading from six to sixteen years old

I wanted to be a soldier, I wanted to be a swan.
I wanted to be stored in a cupboard, I wanted to learn myself.
I wanted to smell of dust.
I wanted to escape at night, I wanted my teachers to cry.
I wanted to live in a cellar, I wanted to survive.
I wanted to be spoken out loud.
I wanted to be unsuitable for children, I wanted to be rude.
I wanted to stand on the sill at night, I wanted the moon.
I did not want to sleep. I wanted to know where the story went,
    which lines were mine.
I didn't want to be Christmas, I wanted snow.
I wanted to drift in dark lanes, I wanted silence.
I wanted to know myself off by heart.
I didn't want to be a doll. I wanted to be teddy, to be soft, I wanted
    muscles.
I wanted to be a cat, in an alley, I wanted to sing.
I didn't want to be the sea. I didn't want to be a place that people
    visited. I didn't want anyone to lie down.
I wanted to be a big house where I could wander. I wanted stairways
    that nobody knew. I wanted to be a corridor with many rooms,
    a Great Hall with the fire gone out.
I wanted to be an old bottle, to be in pieces.
I wanted to be mountain, I wanted to be very high. I wanted heather,
    to write myself, to be pulled up by the roots. I wanted blood.
I wanted to float in dark water with the fires all behind me. I wanted
    to be complicated and very sad.
I wanted to be a map, I wanted to find myself. I wanted to be lost
    in a park and taken home.
I did not want to be destroyed. I wanted my Grandad to recite me,
    I wanted to be a song.
I wanted cider, I wanted a girl. I wanted to make it rain.

I Ask Monkey How He Sleeps

He tells me that some nights
he is a bright moon
that never sets.

Sometimes, when he sleeps
he sees himself reflected in a lake
and he is beautiful.

Some nights, he has company.
Some nights
there is a forest inside him

and the birds will not settle.
He does not believe in ghosts
but some nights, he is haunted.

Some nights, he is all on fire.
The rain is relentless
and the wind excites him.

Some nights, he is a dark path:
he can hardly make himself out.
Some nights he is tree,

he can't lie down.
Oh Monkey, please hold me.
Tonight there are tigers.

I cannot close my eyes.

The Impact of Neglect on the Developing Brain

Dreams:
you can't find your mother.

A series of rooms
one after the other

each smelling of urine
and dust.

And of course
there are ghosts –

you fear them like murder.
By night, there are spiders and mice.

Then sleep is a space
with no air. It's too hot.

All of your words
have been sucked out.

The books on the shelves
are rotten. You read them.

You almost forgot that door,
how the corridor leads you outside.

In the yard, how small you are.
How heavy the sky and the rain.

It's all falling
around your ears.

And the rabbits are still in their hutches
and no one has fed them for years.

Why Did the Monkey Cross the Road?

Because it was the chicken's day off/ because he missed the chicken and wanted to see her/ because he was worried he'd offended her/ because he was afraid something terrible had happened to her.

Because he'd forgotten where he was going and why/ because he was alone for the first six months of his life/ because his mother was cloth and she'd loved him/ because there never even was a chicken.

Because there were demons on his side of the street/ because he had not slept for three days straight/ because no side of the road was right/ because he wanted to get to the bar.

Because he needed to keep on moving/ because he was looking for something just something/ because it gave him the illusion of agency/ because feeling like this was intolerable.

Because he no longer belonged to the pack/ because he wanted to be taken to a place of safety/ because he was lonely/ because he was hungry/ to get to the other side.

Monkey Talks About Self Injury

When he bites himself, he says, he belongs to a tradition
dating back thousands of years.
It is possible he is in cave paintings, though this is undecided.
He is certainly in the Bible, and all major religions.

Monkey is fascinated by Rose of Lima: her fasting, her crown
    of thorns.
She was the most beautiful of all the flowers, he informs me.
Monkey does not believe in God, but he feels strongly
that science lacks imagination and humanity.

He weeps when he reads of self-inflicted wounds in the trenches.
The removal of finger-joints in indigenous cultures
makes him shudder: though he understands the desire
to express grief, he is easily triggered.

Liposuction distresses him terribly, as do piercings.
He can only imagine, he tells me, the horrors that women
endure. We have not discussed waxing, but he is aware
of sunbeds and bleaching. He talks

of Adverse Childhood Experiences, neglect and self-hatred.
I feel there's an elephant in the room,
but it's late, and neither of us wants to name it. Even as I write
Monkey is weeping and rocking

whilst he reads of the consequences of smoking.
I am placing a block on all information relating to suicide,
obesity, alcohol and drugs. Also botox and cage-fighting.
We will return to these subjects in due course

Monkey Writes a Story About God

He lives in the sky
in flashes of horrible light.
He is cruel in the name of love

and there is a baby.
He throws his own son in a pit;
there is no way out.

Monkey is writing his tale
and it hurts.
His story is a surface with no grip,

no branches to climb up.
His poems are sharp wires
and they sting.

The words are small paws –
they leave a trail of blood across the page
and the mess is terrible.

Monkey gives his God unseeing eyes.
He writes demons to scare him.
and no arms to hold him.

Oh my Monkey.
These lines are the bars of a cage.
Now turn the page.

Monkey Joins a Dating App

1. I require a relationship
within 500 miles. I do not believe in God
or pets. I am athletic and very hirsute.

2. I am passionate
about grasshoppers, rain,
keeping warm, and sex from behind.

3. I am grateful for not being dead,
for my good teeth. For the river
and whatever there is in the fridge.

4. The five things I can't live without
are love. And water.

5. Please swipe me. I am excellent
at making children. I avoid inbreeding,
I can fish for ants with a stick.

6. Though I do not own my own car
I am community-minded.
I enjoy making new friends

7. and also sex. I am good at climbing trees.

Self Portrait as Monkey Getting Drunk

When I first drank that stuff –
there was a hopeful sensation on my tongue
and my heart was thirsty.

Then the little monkeys inside me all laid down
and my head was a kind place
and welcomed me home.

I learnt of my special powers.
I could speak any language, I could sing;
I was confident in my body, women loved me

and suddenly, I was at sea
and she was all of the sunrise that filled me
and she was the shore.

She was a forest, I was lost there
and my chest was a field full of light,
a river ran through it.

There were high winds;
the trees were falling
and the stone across my throat was rolled away.

When I look at her

says Monkey
all the doors in my head
swing open

and the lights are on.
There are new rooms inside my house
and the river is silent.

There's sunshine over the moor
and though it's a terrible year
there are two horses.

When I look at her, there's a low owl
hunting by evening.
All the voices in the forest are still.

When she holds me,
I'm first violin.
I'm first in the race, I'm flying,

none of my bones is aching –
I'm getting the hang of this –
when she kisses me,

I am the Chilean miners
reaching the air.
And though she's a country I've never visited

I'm picking up the language
quick.
I'm on the deck of a ship at night

and the moon is out
and the engines are roaring
and it's full steam, full steam ahead.

Monkey Teaches Me Map-reading Skills

Show me where you are on this map
says Monkey. I tell him it's impossible.
I lost all of my navigational skills as a result
of a terrible shock
and anyway, I met this woman for lunch
and she took me to a hut in a forest,
I have no idea where, and we lived there for years –
we drank from a spring and built fires;

we were happy. She went to the shops in January
and I fell asleep on the floor
and woke up in summer. There were butterflies
and our children pronounced them in Spanish.
All that I know is – this morning
we were somewhere high up on a moor.
Believe me, I have no idea where I am, Monkey:

when I first met her
we stood very close on the Tube
although there were seats.
We were trying to get back to the hotel
and her fingers were inbetween mine
and her eyes were a green shade of brown
and we were lost. But Monkey insists

so I show him.
I am here – where a river meets the sea –
I am sitting by the fire, I am high on the moor,
I am in her bed, I am waking with her,
I have travelled a long way to be with her.
See here Monkey, I know where I am exactly,
I am in a hut, in a forest, I am in Love.

What the Goldfish Taught Me About Love

That goldfish get lonely.
That goldfish make poor decisions when drunk.
That goldfish can be aggressive, though not often.
That a happy goldfish shines.
That lethargy is a sign of emotional distress,
that depression is no joke, that sex is exhausting.

That gender is controversial and ambiguous.
That goldfish are not ordinary, especially to themselves.
That a goldfish will die in a small tank.
That the water can be toxic
but escape is lethal.
That keeping goldfish requires some care.

That the water is not clear when you are in it.
That you can see yourself reflected in the sky.
That there are lights, and the tank seems endless.
That there is a value in repetition.
That repetition enchants the brain,
that pebbles are beautiful.

That you shouldn't make assumptions about goldfish.
That goldfish memory is better than commonly believed.
That goldfish swim in circles because of the bowl.
That the castle is huge. That you go there
not because you forgot it – that you want it
even though you know all of its rooms.

Self-portrait as Hermaphroditus entering the water

Love is the name for our pursuit of wholeness,
for our desire to be complete.

PLATO

Love lived in the trees
and it waited. It flowed in the water.

Love hung in the branches
like the moon.

You were strong, you were slim.
You were the sun.

Love was a pool
and you wanted to swim.

Love stripped you
and you waded in.

You were naked.
There were no stones.

Love was clear as a dream
and you were in it.

Silence and sunlight.
Love had god on its side

and no one
could save you from it.

It was hungry
and swallowed you whole.

Fish trembled.
The lilies were open wide.

Night Swimming, Derwentwater

Each lake is a page
we have not written on.
The mist is breath

suspended. Stars shiver.
There's a ghost
of a winter moon.

It is late December:
the fish are hiding.
They hang in the shadows

like dreams.
We are half in the water
which stretches forever

in the moment
that feels like flight.
The cold is a hurt

we return to, over and over.
The darkness is memory
and reeds.

The hills are as bright as paper.
The water is quieter
than snow.

There are black things
between the trees
and the paths are hidden

but the sky
is a language of stars
and the stars are beneath us

and the moon is in pieces
and there's nothing to stop us from falling
but our arms.

Love as an Adder in Grizedale

It was shockingly clear.
Though we were in a forest
and the sun was lost in the mist

and there were rivers
and ferns like fossils uncoiling
and long walls snaking

and everything green was grey
and blue and purple and yellow
and never silent or still

it wasn't a grass snake
so obvious and motionless
we almost fell on it.

This was a fuse
and I wanted to hold it.
This was a nerve

and I wanted to touch it.
I bent my head near.
Its tongue was a warning. Beware

of the crow and the fox and the badger,
beware of the grass
and the boot of the rambler;

beware of dark places, beware of the stranger.
I was with my sister
and I did not see the danger.

Beware of the sunlight.
Beware the familiar.

Love as DIY

There's a crack in the wall
and I'm marking its progress.
The carpet is stained and the paper is peeling.
There's a nest in the chimney; five slates need replacing.
In the dark, I have terrible thoughts.

Two beams are rotten. I'm scared of the ceiling,
the lawn gone to seed and the trees in the garden,
how the boards creak and moan
when I'm pacing the kitchen
regretting my bodged repairs:

the sag in the gutter, the dripping of water,
the pattern of damp
like a map on the plaster,
the unpainted frames and the gaps by the window,
the boiler that keeps me awake.

I'm afraid of the rain
and the mice in the cellar. The groundwater rising,
the slight smell of burning. Afraid of the wind
and the broken slates flying.
I'm afraid of the woman I love

and the slump in my roof and that patch on the rafters
and the ivy that loosens the bricks with its fingers.
There's a crack in the wall
and I'm tracking its progress.
I'll go down in flames or I'll go down by inches.

My Girlfriend Did Not Believe in Ghosts

though they walked heavily through our rooms
and made the floor shake

though we were under attack
though there was a darkness

though the door was pulled from its hinges
though nothing moved

though they banged on the walls by our bed
though the priest came

though my mother woke each night
who art in heaven

though there was whispering
though my brother saw lights in the dark

though I woke to a man in my room
though I looked him in the eye and walked away

though I have lived with them all of my life
though I know myself

though strangers asked who was upstairs
though no one was

though I made it through the end of times
and I found feathers

though nobody touched me
though they would not leave me alone

Love as a Poem

We were a poem. Do you remember?
We were its crossings-out, its contradictions.
We didn't care – we broke the rules,
we knew so little
of form or style. We wrote ourselves

in bedrooms late at night
and didn't ask for recognition –
we were open to multiple interpretations
and all of them were right. Yes, we were happy,
we were poetry, it was beautiful –

we were lights in the trees, late evening;
we were a heron, we meant something
very profound, and we meant nothing.
Some days, you poured out of me
and I could not stop.

I wrote my best for you, I stayed up late;
I was satisfied
with the results. I wanted to hear you
out loud – oh
we were so loud!

And there were times we were blank despair.
I was a story
that went on too long; I lost your attention.
I lost my voice. No matter how hard I worked,
you wouldn't come.

We were a villanelle; we kept on going
in circles. We were epic:
heroic and tragic, we delivered long speeches.
Then we were lament
and elegy. We were sad.

And our ending was sudden, and bad.

The *Titanic* Reflects on the Recent Ending of a Long-term Relationship

Though I never believed we were unsinkable,
I thought we'd make it.
Stars shone.
Music played often, there was dancing.

I was not unsuited to the elements;
I was strong.
Though I carried disaster within me,
in the end it came from outside.

Who would have thought it,
that perfect night?
Though the sea was a cloud of stars,
there was no moon.

Your words were ice –
they broke me.
They tore a hole down my side,
I was gutted.

Thousands of plates smashed inside me.
The engines stopped.
We were so many hours from help
and the stars were so bright.

Sweetheart, the orchestra did its best
but they all drowned.

Self-portrait as Claude Cahun and Marcel Moore

We were art. We were collage. We were in pieces.
We were stuck back together. We were lovers and sisters.
We were a book though few people read us.
We were before our time.

We were a poem and a picture and sculpture.
We were angel and vampire and dandy and soldier.
We were all genres, we lived on the borders.
We were not easy to understand.

We were artists from Paris. We were very strange ladies –
we were an act of resistance and madness.
We were alarmingly close
and extremely courageous. We were Mr and Mrs

and I was an image and you were a camera
and you were the letter and I was a writer
and we were an island in summer and winter
and we were at war but we never surrendered –

we both burned together. We were one,
we were many. We were family and army.
You were my lover, my other. You left me
and I was the sky and the sea, I was empty.

I come from Kergulen

The wind here is relentless
and its name is Desolation.

There are no trees and little to eat.
It is 2,501 miles to civilisation.

These are the remotest islands in all the world.
Snow falls often, even in summer.

Here, you must be self-sufficient.
You must be muscled; you must laugh at penguins.

Humans have tried and failed
and left their ruins behind.

The cliffs are shattered. The world is far away
but the moon is perfect.

Stars shine in millions, there are birds
and I speak the language of weather.

I have faith that storms pass quickly,
sun will rise.

I would feed you eggs
if I could

but the wind has blown you away.
Oh my sweetness, please return.

There is no postal service
but I miss you.

Sometimes the only thing I do
is wait for dawn.

Love as a SatNav

Love is a permanent presence, it keeps you company.
It can speak in many voices,
but you pay for it. Sometimes
you pick it up cheap.
Love guides you around diversions; it saves you.

It does not alter
when it alteration finds – it is the star.
When it is dark, love shines brightly.
It is not infallible. Sometimes, it takes you
up entirely unsuitable roads: it leaves you

on the edge of a drop, in deep shit.
Love is not a reliable book;
you should disregard it.
It insists it has brought you to the correct destination
but you are stuck

where you never wanted to be.
A roundabout in Pontefract, for example
with love repeating the same unhelpful instructions.
You are lost. You have no idea
how you got there or –

turn around when possible –
where the hell you should head to
next.

Love as a Global Pandemic

March 2020

Love as a rumour.
Love as a growing sense of unease.
Love as local transmission, love as a headline.

Love as contagion, love as severe disruption.
Love as flight. Love as the closing
of borders, love as home.

Love as beyond belief. Love as exhaustion.
Love as breathlessness, love as fever.
Love as a permanent knot,

love as a panic attack.
Love as a basic essential, love as delivery.
Love as a proportionate response, love as no cure.

Love as keeping your distance, love as prayer.
Love as a park you can't sit in,
love as birds.

Love as an overwhelming situation.
Love as a state of emergency,
love as bankruptcy, love as lies.

Love as a series of terrible decisions,
love as a test. Love as lack of protection,
love as no chance.

Love as a critical condition, love as
high-dependency. Love as intensive care.
Love as recovery.

Love as human-to-human transmission.
Love as a whole town clapping.
Love as a full glass of whisky, love as an empty sky.

What the Moon Taught Me About Love

April 2020

I think it must be one of my earliest memories*
orange squash, crêpe paper streamers,
pale crisps in paper dishes.
Let's say it's then that snow starts falling:
bright flakes drift in the Burnley darkness.
I remember a perfect moon,
the night outside complete and endless
and we sing because the grown-ups tell us
that Santa will hear us –
and sure enough, we hear bells,
our faces pressed to the plate-glass windows
and though I'm expecting a sleigh, we see torches
and the air is a charge and it flows through our bodies.
Lights on the field and they're heading towards us.
There's no reason to remember this today
when summer creeps into the year too early –
the redcurrant blossom has started to wither
and the bees getting fat but the ducks going hungry
and the sky is painfully blue and empty
and the lambs are growing up fast
and the weeks are months but the hours pass quickly
and night falls silent as snow on the valley
and once I was small and entirely happy,
once there were lights on a field in Burnley.
And the moon tonight is very lonely.

Total Social Isolation in Monkeys

May 2020

After a while, says Monkey, I learned to accept it.
I stopped trying to climb the walls.
Time became malleable
and largely irrelevant.
There's no pressure to sleep at night.
When I find my own pace,
the day is a lake I can float in quite gently.
And each day is incredibly long
and surprisingly busy.
I am a house with many rooms
and the rooms are all filled
with fruit. It's okay to be insane –
some of the visions are pleasant,
my thoughts are extraordinary.
I touch myself very adeptly
and the walls are safety.
It's not as silent as you might expect.
I recite poetry in various forms,
I speak with demons. I am learning
to embrace my own company.
Though lacking resources, I have time.
There's a great deal in here left to learn.

Love at the William Thompson Recreation Centre

June 2020

where we were children and thin and unclean,
where reception sold goggles and sachets of Vosene,
where the turnstiles counted us in.
Where our hands were sticky, where men were a mystery,
where we could not enter the gym.

Where we were men and we smelt like horses,
where we were horses and ran through the showers
where water burned in our eyes and our noses
where we clung to the edges and hung on each other
where the room was a pool full of sound.

Where we pissed in the same pool we swam in together
where water was rain I could stand in forever
where we undressed, where we were uncovered
where we were inches away from each other,
where old people danced with their hands on each other.

Where gym teachers placed their strong hands to correct us
where the springboard could not make me fly.
Where we were birds and we flocked close together,
where we were cattle and herded together,
where we were fish and we swam with each other –

where we learned to open our eyes underwater,
where the water was each other's bodies and voices
when there was so little distance between us.

Lorry Driver

(after Eiléan Ní Chuilleanáin)

When all this is over, I will take to the road
where the day starts at 3am
and conversation is largely a matter
of country music on late-night stations.

I want to learn a new language:
to blow my doors off, to be southbound
and hammer-down through Europe,
to drive through centuries of forest,
the memories of trees in the dark.

I intend to travel in straight lines,
to be shocked by the colour each morning,
to stop only where the services are worth it.
I want to be stalked by wolves,
to drive on bridges that might not hold.

I won't hurry. On the high tracks over La Paz
I will take it steady
where dusty plastic flowers mark the graves.
I will be adept with a mallet and hammer
and the weather will be my story.

The world will shrink in my mirror,
storms will approach me.
I want life to drive towards me all lit up.
I want to be awake through the night
with hundreds of miles still to go.

The Garden of Earthly Delights

Back then, I was the moon.
I shone, I was perfect
and the trees were all heavy with fruit.

There was a heat between us
and it was divine. Your hair was long
and you smelt of sun.

Every word of this is the truth –
how a lion is filled with desire,
how women are fish, you can swim there.

How two people together are flower,
how flowers bloom from us.
How we carry a beast on our shoulders,

how we are birds.
We were so hungry back then –
do you remember?

We kept on eating the fruit
and I do not regret it
though a city burned in me

and there was rubble;
though the sun abandoned the sky.
Back then

we were not ashamed of our skin.
We lay in the grass and you smelt of sun.
And what happened between us was holy.

Everything Is a Gift.

The gift of the city at night.
The gift of the light on a knife
held towards you, the gift of two men.

The gift of the ground to catch you,
the gift of flowers.
The gift of a boot in your face,

the gift of stars.
The gift of trees and their silence,
the gift of blood.

The gift of time, how it swallows you,
how it delivers you
to the other side.

The gift of the cheekbone and jaw.
The gift of the moon which was looking elsewhere,
the gift of sirens.

The gift of the witness of cars,
of a thick coat with padding,
the gift of strong bones.

The gift of helplessness.
The gift of the instinct for life,
how the scream is the language of life,

the gift of flight –
how the clouds were so solid they could hold you,
how storms were forming.

How a young girl fell into a well
and survived. How twelve boys were lost
in a cave, how a man died for them.

The gift of a bomb in the face,
the gift of darkness.
The gift of the stars all around you,

the gift of the moon.

You couldn't make it up

The doctor is laying his hands on me. He is sorry
for my suffering and asks Jesus to heal me.
But Jesus is still in bed. He sleeps
at the end of the dorm, in a woman's body
he shares with Satan.

Satan is outside Sandra's cubicle.
She can see his shadow through the curtains
and he looks like spiders.
I sleep next door.
Christina Baxter of the Baxter Soup Empire

sleeps next to me. We smoke in bed;
we sail in our beds like boats.
Everything is very meaningful.
Tommy has stabbed himself
and now he is dead. Silly Tommy.
If I don't take off my coat, I'll be safe.

All the songs are about us
and they hurt. We are delicate.
Trees mean freedom. There's no natural light
but the angels keep sending us feathers;
they have not forgotten us.

And if there's a message in the pool cue
it's that we're broken. If there's a message in
the door, it's that we're strong. This is fact.
Everything will be all right.
Not a word of this is a lie.

Information for Survivors of Sexual Abuse and Rape

– based on a leaflet available at safeline.org.uk

Though *sexual abuse takes many forms*,
salmon will find their way home, I have seen them
leaping up falls, there was nothing calm
about them, the current and cold
could not stop them, they were sky-born
and silver. *There are many reasons*

survivors do not tell.
Most whale song cannot be heard
by the human ear, yet it travels for
ten thousand miles, which is more than
the world, and it sounds like dreaming,
like wolf and bird.

Flashbacks are recollections from the past
and in Tromsø, the sun will not rise from
November to January.
You may feel you are going crazy
but the worst is over,
and though you are very afraid

when their oxygen tank blew apart
a quarter of a million miles from earth
the crew of Apollo 13 made it back
unharmed. *Remember to breathe.*
The Shaman travels beyond the ordinary
and an animal walks beside you,

you are power
and though *you couldn't remove yourself*
from the situation you were in,
there are 7.422 billion people in the world
and rising, you are not alone.
The sun will not set in Tromsø

between May and June
but it's the winter that people love
when the ice glows blue
and the night is a colour of its own.
Sometimes lights will dance in the sky
and though it's minus thirty

it will be enough to warm you,
to sustain you, enough
to convince you to stay.

Other than Personality Disorder, what term could you use to describe these people?

These people are Arctic Terns
who launch their tiny weight into the wind.
Their problem is winter,

their problem is weather; they avoid storms
by taking the largest detours to find land.
They are abundant.

These people fly between poles
and they sleep on the wing – they spiral,
their endurance is legendary.

They will bite your head
if they have to: they will draw blood.
They sing a high song of alarm

and they know two summers;
They have been studied and trapped
and tracked in their journeys,

these people are remarkable –
they have magnets inside their heads,
they go where they have to.

They know the glow of the snow
on the water, the sea as a glimmer,
the mountains as blades in the sky.

And they are the subject of various papers.
And life is harsh, and days are endless.

Self-portrait as Hermaphroditus coming out of the water

Let's say it was love made me like this.
Say it was luck. Let's say it was roses.
My back was broad and I had strong shoulders.
Let's say it was in the stars.

Let's say I was led there by no one
and the forest was lit by the moon.

Let's say I was young and I didn't know better.
My father's son and my mother's daughter.
Let's say that no one called me monster.
Let's say that it didn't hurt.

I was fruit on the tree and you loved me.
Let's say I was not what you thought.

I went with the current and I did not fight it.
There was a song in my head
and no one could hear it.
Let's say that science will never explain it

those things in the water we don't understand yet.
Creatures we have not named.

Let's say we are creatures. Let's say we are helpless.
Let's say it is easy and hard.
Let's say it was doves. Let's say it was roses.
Let's say it was love

made me like this – and luck.
Let's say it was in the stars.

Monkey Invites Me to Imagine

I am walking in snow for the first time
and my paws are bare.

The fields seem endless
and I cannot make sense of the sky.

The air is rapid and quiet. It burns
but Monkey is peaceful.

He bids me notice
that sheep are not actually white,

that some pain is worth it.
He does not tell me

to put my boots on, not to eat it.
When you come late to snow,

says Monkey, you will always be ready
to stand under the moon

to watch it fall.
Sometimes, I don't know which of us

is Monkey. Especially now
when he is leading me

carefully up to my room
and we stop by the high window

so that I can stare at the snow.
Look how beautiful it is!

For this night at least,
no harm will come to us.

The Chronicles of Narnia

Somewhere, there's another world
behind a door you've been knocking on
since you were young.

It's not that you want to escape your life –
just that somewhere, very close by,
in a room you've never explored,

there's a forest where snow falls
in the warm light cast by a lamp.
The moon hangs in a Northern sky,

the stream is frozen.
There are thousands and thousands of stars.
You don't need a key, or a ring

and there's no point in knocking:
every heart is a secret door.
One day, you'll walk right through

and you'll be there.
Perhaps a shadow in the trees will approach you.
You'll feel powerful and brave, and very small.

Then your heart will be lion and mountains,
an acre of blue flowers blooming
and you'll stride into a world

you always believed in
because there always was bright moss
and birdsong and river

and stars – oh my love
though I didn't know how to reach you
all my life, I knew you were there.

If Love is Snow

then I want to be the kind of person
who is always glad when it snows.
when the air comes alive
and you wake to a different light.

If Love is snow
I always want to say YES to sledging
even when I'm eighty and my hips hurt,
even if it's late

and the moon is over the fields.
And if a snowball slaps me – whack –
In the back of my head,
I don't want to be the kind of person

who storms off, muttering about kids.
If Love is snow
I want handfuls of the stuff for myself.
I don't care if it hurts

or if the trains are cancelled. I don't mind
being late for work,
I want the whole town to wake to snow
to run out, our eyes full of wonder,

ready to jump right in.
I want to stay the kind of person
who finds snow beautiful,
even when I fall.

Things I find attractive in a person

Bad weather. To have the whole world
in your chest, to feel it spin. To be a coiled thing.
To be Venice and Paris
and not Berlin. To be single
or not single; to need me.

Flight. To wake me up
with your rain, to ruin my ceiling.
To swim against currents
to spawn, to be endangered.
To be a place of hard work

to be comfortable. To have a bed
for a belly, to let me lie there.
To be a lake – to be swimmable in.
To have wings, or strong arms,
or fire. To be garden,

to be high wall, to be the key.
To be a whole country –
to have borders, wire fences,
to bid me enter.
To make me welcome there. To let me stay.

Instructions for Care

If it becomes apparent that I'm in trouble
please take me to a National Trust property
with gift shop and café
and free samples of various preserves.

I will be happy there
with fruit curd and chutney
and a selection of books by Monty Don.
It will set me right.

Here are pencils and thread to mend me.
I am calm. In the company
of short-haired ladies
in floral trousers, I know myself.

My heart is a medieval depiction of hell
and I can only apologise
for the state of me – how I am always naked
with arrows right through me,

how I am strapped to the edge of a knife.
Take me to a room that smells of butter,
I want shortbread rounds.
I don't want to think about death anymore –

I want to consider the life cycle of waterfowl.
I want a family egg hunt
with a fabulous chocolate prize.
Nothing can bring her back

like an exhibition of wildlife photography.
By the edge of a shallow lake
I will learn to knit. Sometimes
there is just too much pain.

Day after a migraine

You shouldn't smoke, especially the day after
a migraine. I smell of coal-tar, very clean.
There's a small room inside the self
a long way from pain – I can float there, boxed and
untethered. I hear a choir, so clear I want to
remember their names. My floors are freshly clean.

There's tea on the hob, my scorched kettle.
The neighbour plays tin-whistle upstairs;
he leaves wood on my doorstep. *Do you
want me to saw it?* It's okay, it's okay, I want the sun.
My ex calls to check I'm okay. I'm okay, though I still
shake. I want to say thank you, but we're not like that.

A box of free stuff on the street, the sign says *Free stuff.*
Two of my friends are waiting for their mothers to die.
Every migraine, I remember my mother's last days,
how she bled from her eyes. Of course I can't get
beyond it. There was an hour of sunshine, there was
blossom; I cried because she could not see it.

Whoever asked me then are you okay got the full story.
Somewhere across the world, my sister is reading this.
I wake in the night and look out at a desert,
at a small town mapped in lights: a main street, a road
leading to nowhere. My glass stares at me
with empty eyes, it is very tired. There's no wind tonight

and I am weatherless. There will be sunshine again.
At the top of Stake Pass, I found a tent, abandoned.
A campfire. I could see then, for miles, and I know
that when the zombie apocalypse comes,
this is where I'll pitch up; the sound of the river,
clean water to bathe in each morning. This is how I'll survive.

Monkey Reads William Blake

The Angel that presided o'er my birth
Said, 'Little creature, form'd of Joy & Mirth
'Go love without the help of any Thing on Earth.'

WILLIAM BLAKE

Monkey has developed a fancy for William Blake.
He puts down his book and tells me
that Blake is part monkey

and John Clare, with his exquisitely sensitive eye.
Dogs, he says, are also half monkey.
He explains

to be kicked to the dirt
to know blood at the back of your throat
and not only to want to be touched

but to rage for it –
you must be Monkey.
To be Badger, to live in the night

and still to believe in the sun, to be Cat –
to see in the dark, to be dropped
and to save yourself.

To be Blake, who hated the cage so much
he rid his brain of it –
to find angels in the street

and take them home –
I think I am starting to understand.
To burn bright with it,

to be naked and scarred? Monkey nods.
I think this is an important moment of connection
but Monkey is already busy.

He is scribbling on the pages of his book
and the full moon is rising
and Monkey is spinning –

the dogs are all howling,
the two of us dancing
and Monkey is grinning.

ACKNOWLEDGEMENTS

The title of this collection is a direct reference to *A General Theory of Love* by Thomas Lewis, Fari Amini and Richard Lannon (Random House, 2000).

Thanks to John Foggin, editor of *When All This Is Over* (Calder Valley Poetry, 2020), where 'Lorry Driver' was first published, and to Candlestick Press, publishers of *Christmas Movies: A Double Bill of Festive Poems*, where 'Chronicles of Narnia' was first published.

The following poems were first published by the 'WRITE where we are now' project (2020), curated by Carol Ann Duffy and the Manchester Writing School in response to the Coronavirus pandemic, and archived by the Manchester Poetry Library: 'Love as a Global Pandemic', 'What the Moon Taught Me About Love', 'Total Social Isolation in Monkeys', 'Love at the William Thompson Recreation Centre' and 'The Garden of Earthly Delights'.

The following poems were written as part of a residency at the 10th International Congress of the International Society for the Prevention of Child Abuse and Neglect 2018: 'Information for Survivors of Sexual Abuse and Rape', 'Child Protection Policy' and 'Other than Personality Disorder, what term could you use to describe these people?' 'Information for Survivors of Sexual Abuse and Rape' draws directly by a leaflet produced by Safeline, available at www.safeline.org.uk. 'If Love is Snow' was written in response to poetry produced by the young people of the Five Rivers Childcare Family, as part of National Care Day 2021.

The following poems were written during a residency at *Beneath this Mask*, a Claude Cahun exhibition at the Hebden Bridge Arts Festival 2018: 'Self-portrait as Claude Cahun and Marcel Moore', 'Self-portrait as Hermaphroditus coming out of the water' and 'Self-portrait as Hermaphroditus entering the water'. The opening of 'What the Moon Taught Me About Love' draws on a line from 'Lollipops Are for Winners' by Adrian Salmon.

The title of 'An Empirical Examination of the Stage Theory of Grief' references a paper by that name by P. Maciejewski et al (2007) published in the *Journal of the American Medical Association*, 297 (7): 716-23. The title of 'A Psychological Study of The Strange Situation' references *Patterns of attachment: A psychological study of the strange situation* by Mary D. Salter Ainsworth et al (Routledge, 1979).

The author acknowledges a debt of gratitude to the following sources: J. Armstrong (2003), *Conditions of Love: The Philosophy of Intimacy* (Penguin Books, 2003); Julian Barnes, *Levels of Life* (Jonathan Cape, 2013); and Deborah Blum, *Love at Goon Park: Harry Harlow and the Science of Affection* (John Wiley and Sons, 2002).